EMMANUEL JOSEPH

The Crypto Trader's Handbook: Strategies for Digital Markets

Copyright © 2025 by Emmanuel Joseph

All rights reserved. No part of this publication may be reproduced, stored or transmitted in any form or by any means, electronic, mechanical, photocopying, recording, scanning, or otherwise without written permission from the publisher. It is illegal to copy this book, post it to a website, or distribute it by any other means without permission.

First edition

This book was professionally typeset on Reedsy.
Find out more at reedsy.com

Contents

1	Chapter 1: Introduction to Cryptocurrency Trading	1
2	Chapter 2: Understanding Market Trends and Analysis	3
3	Chapter 3: Developing a Trading Strategy	5
4	Chapter 4: Risk Management and Trading Psychology	7
5	Chapter 5: Technical Analysis Tools and Indicators	9
6	Chapter 6: Fundamentals of Blockchain Technology	11
7	Chapter 7: Navigating Cryptocurrency Exchanges	13
8	Chapter 8: The Role of Stablecoins in Crypto Trading	15
9	Chapter 9: Leveraging DeFi in Crypto Trading	17
10	Chapter 10: Security Best Practices for Crypto Traders	19
11	Chapter 11: Tax Implications and Legal Considerations	21
12	Chapter 12: Future Trends and Innovations in Crypto Trading	23

1

Chapter 1: Introduction to Cryptocurrency Trading

Cryptocurrency trading has emerged as a lucrative yet volatile arena in the financial markets. This chapter introduces readers to the fundamental concepts of cryptocurrency and the basics of trading. It delves into the history of digital currencies, explaining how Bitcoin, the first cryptocurrency, paved the way for an entirely new asset class. Additionally, this chapter highlights the core principles of trading, including market psychology, risk management, and the importance of a well-thought-out trading plan.

The exponential growth of cryptocurrencies has attracted a diverse group of investors and traders. From individual hobbyists to institutional players, the crypto market offers opportunities for everyone. However, it is essential to recognize the high-risk nature of this market. This chapter emphasizes the need for thorough research and a disciplined approach to trading. By understanding the market's complexities and dynamics, traders can better navigate the volatile landscape and make informed decisions.

As we move deeper into the world of cryptocurrency trading, it is crucial to understand the tools and resources available. This chapter provides an overview of various trading platforms, wallets, and analytical tools that can aid in making better trading decisions. It also discusses the importance of staying updated with the latest news and developments in the crypto space. Being well-informed is key to staying ahead in this fast-paced market.

Finally, this chapter touches upon the legal and regulatory aspects of cryptocurrency trading. As governments worldwide grapple with how to regulate digital assets, traders must be aware of the evolving legal landscape. Understanding the regulatory environment can help traders avoid potential pitfalls and ensure they operate within the confines of the law. By the end of this chapter, readers will have a solid foundation to build their cryptocurrency trading journey.

2

Chapter 2: Understanding Market Trends and Analysis

To succeed in cryptocurrency trading, one must master the art of market analysis. This chapter delves into the various types of market analysis, including technical, fundamental, and sentiment analysis. Technical analysis involves studying historical price data and chart patterns to predict future price movements. This section covers essential tools and indicators, such as moving averages, RSI, and MACD, which traders can use to identify trends and make informed decisions.

Fundamental analysis, on the other hand, focuses on evaluating the intrinsic value of a cryptocurrency. This involves examining factors such as the underlying technology, team, partnerships, and market adoption. By understanding these elements, traders can make better long-term investment decisions. This chapter provides practical examples and case studies to illustrate how fundamental analysis can be applied to the crypto market.

Sentiment analysis is another critical component of market analysis. It involves gauging the overall mood and sentiment of market participants. This can be achieved by monitoring social media, news outlets, and forums to identify trends and potential market-moving events. This chapter explains how traders can use sentiment analysis to their advantage, particularly during periods of heightened market volatility.

Combining these three types of analysis can provide a comprehensive view of the market and help traders make more informed decisions. This chapter emphasizes the importance of developing a robust analytical framework and continuously refining it based on market conditions. By mastering market analysis, traders can better anticipate price movements and capitalize on trading opportunities.

3

Chapter 3: Developing a Trading Strategy

A well-defined trading strategy is crucial for success in the cryptocurrency market. This chapter explores various trading strategies, including day trading, swing trading, and long-term investing. Each strategy has its pros and cons, and traders must choose one that aligns with their risk tolerance, time commitment, and financial goals. This chapter provides detailed examples and step-by-step guides for implementing each strategy.

Day trading involves making multiple trades within a single day to capitalize on short-term price movements. This strategy requires a high level of discipline, quick decision-making, and an in-depth understanding of technical analysis. This section covers the key elements of a successful day trading strategy, including setting entry and exit points, managing risk, and using stop-loss orders to protect capital.

Swing trading, on the other hand, focuses on capturing price movements over a few days to weeks. This strategy allows traders to take advantage of short- to medium-term trends without the pressure of monitoring the market constantly. This chapter discusses the essential components of a swing trading strategy, such as identifying trend reversals, using support and resistance levels, and employing technical indicators to confirm trade signals.

Long-term investing involves holding onto a cryptocurrency for an extended period, often years, to benefit from its potential growth. This strategy requires a thorough understanding of the fundamentals and a strong conviction in the project's long-term prospects. This section provides guidance on selecting promising projects, diversifying investments, and managing portfolio risk.

By the end of this chapter, readers will have a solid grasp of various trading strategies and the tools needed to implement them effectively. Developing a well-thought-out trading plan and sticking to it can significantly improve the chances of success in the volatile world of cryptocurrency trading.

4

Chapter 4: Risk Management and Trading Psychology

Risk management is a critical aspect of successful cryptocurrency trading. This chapter delves into the various risk management techniques that traders can employ to protect their capital and minimize losses. Key concepts such as position sizing, stop-loss orders, and diversification are discussed in detail. By understanding and applying these principles, traders can better manage their risk and improve their overall trading performance.

Trading psychology is another essential element of successful trading. Emotions such as fear, greed, and overconfidence can significantly impact decision-making and lead to poor trading outcomes. This chapter explores the psychological aspects of trading and provides practical tips for maintaining a disciplined and focused mindset. Techniques such as mindfulness, journaling, and setting realistic goals can help traders stay grounded and make more rational decisions.

This chapter also highlights the importance of developing a trading routine and sticking to it. A well-structured routine can help traders stay organized, maintain consistency, and avoid impulsive decisions. This section provides guidance on creating a daily trading plan, setting aside time for research and analysis, and periodically reviewing and adjusting the trading strategy based on performance.

Finally, this chapter addresses the common pitfalls and challenges that traders may encounter in the cryptocurrency market. By understanding these potential obstacles and developing strategies to overcome them, traders can better navigate the volatile crypto landscape. This chapter emphasizes the importance of continuous learning and self-improvement to stay ahead in the ever-evolving world of cryptocurrency trading.

5

Chapter 5: Technical Analysis Tools and Indicators

Technical analysis is a cornerstone of cryptocurrency trading. This chapter provides a comprehensive overview of the essential tools and indicators traders use to analyze market trends and price movements. Key indicators such as Moving Averages, Relative Strength Index (RSI), Bollinger Bands, and Moving Average Convergence Divergence (MACD) are explained in detail. Each indicator is illustrated with examples to show how traders can use them to identify potential entry and exit points.

The chapter also explores advanced technical analysis techniques, including Fibonacci retracements, Elliot Wave Theory, and Ichimoku Cloud. These tools can help traders gain deeper insights into market dynamics and anticipate price movements more accurately. By understanding and applying these advanced techniques, traders can enhance their analytical skills and make more informed decisions.

Chart patterns are another crucial aspect of technical analysis. This chapter covers various chart patterns, such as head and shoulders, double tops and bottoms, and triangles, which can signal potential trend reversals or continuations. By recognizing these patterns, traders can better anticipate market movements and develop effective trading strategies.

Finally, this chapter emphasizes the importance of combining multiple indicators and tools to create a well-rounded analysis. Relying on a single indicator can be misleading, so traders should use a combination of tools to confirm signals and increase the accuracy of their predictions. By mastering technical analysis, traders can gain a significant edge in the competitive world of cryptocurrency trading.

6

Chapter 6: Fundamentals of Blockchain Technology

A solid understanding of blockchain technology is essential for cryptocurrency traders. This chapter delves into the core concepts of blockchain, including its decentralized nature, consensus mechanisms, and cryptographic principles. By grasping these fundamentals, traders can better appreciate the underlying technology that powers cryptocurrencies and make more informed investment decisions.

This chapter also explores the different types of blockchain networks, such as public, private, and consortium blockchains. Each type has its unique characteristics and use cases, and understanding these distinctions can help traders assess the potential of various projects. Additionally, this chapter covers the concept of smart contracts and how they enable decentralized applications (dApps) to function on blockchain networks.

The chapter also examines the various consensus mechanisms used in blockchain networks, such as Proof of Work (PoW), Proof of Stake (PoS), and Delegated Proof of Stake (DPoS). Each mechanism has its advantages and trade-offs, and understanding these can help traders evaluate the security and scalability of different blockchain projects.

Finally, this chapter highlights the potential of blockchain technology beyond cryptocurrencies. From supply chain management to healthcare and finance, blockchain has the potential to revolutionize various industries. By understanding the broader implications of blockchain technology, traders can better identify long-term investment opportunities in the crypto space.

7

Chapter 7: Navigating Cryptocurrency Exchanges

Cryptocurrency exchanges are the primary platforms for buying and selling digital assets. This chapter provides an in-depth look at the different types of exchanges, including centralized exchanges (CEX), decentralized exchanges (DEX), and hybrid exchanges. Each type of exchange has its pros and cons, and traders must choose one that aligns with their needs and preferences.

Centralized exchanges, such as Binance and Coinbase, offer high liquidity and a wide range of trading pairs. However, they require users to trust the exchange with their funds, which can pose security risks. This chapter discusses the key features of centralized exchanges, including order types, trading fees, and security measures.

Decentralized exchanges, such as Uniswap and SushiSwap, operate without a central authority and allow users to trade directly from their wallets. While DEXs offer enhanced security and privacy, they may have lower liquidity and higher fees compared to CEXs. This chapter explores the advantages and challenges of using decentralized exchanges and provides tips for navigating their unique interfaces.

Hybrid exchanges aim to combine the best features of CEXs and DEXs, offering high liquidity and security while maintaining user control over funds.

This chapter discusses the emerging trend of hybrid exchanges and how they can benefit traders.

Finally, this chapter provides practical tips for choosing the right exchange, creating an account, and managing funds securely. By understanding the different types of exchanges and their features, traders can make more informed decisions and minimize the risks associated with trading on these platforms.

8

Chapter 8: The Role of Stablecoins in Crypto Trading

Stablecoins play a crucial role in the cryptocurrency market by providing a stable value anchor amidst the volatility of digital assets. This chapter explains the concept of stablecoins and how they differ from traditional cryptocurrencies. Stablecoins are typically pegged to a fiat currency, such as the US dollar, and are designed to maintain a stable value.

This chapter explores the different types of stablecoins, including fiat-collateralized, crypto-collateralized, and algorithmic stablecoins. Each type has its unique mechanisms for maintaining stability, and understanding these can help traders choose the right stablecoins for their needs.

Fiat-collateralized stablecoins, such as Tether (USDT) and USD Coin (USDC), are backed by reserves of fiat currency held in a bank account. This chapter discusses the advantages and risks associated with fiat-collateralized stablecoins and how they can be used in trading strategies.

Crypto-collateralized stablecoins, such as Dai (DAI), are backed by reserves of other cryptocurrencies. This chapter explores the mechanisms that ensure the stability of crypto-collateralized stablecoins and their potential use cases in the crypto market.

Algorithmic stablecoins, such as Ampleforth (AMPL), use algorithms to adjust their supply based on market demand. This chapter explains the innovative mechanisms behind algorithmic stablecoins and their potential benefits and challenges.

By understanding the role of stablecoins in crypto trading, traders can better manage their risk and take advantage of arbitrage opportunities. This chapter provides practical examples and case studies to illustrate how stablecoins can be integrated into various trading strategies.

9

Chapter 9: Leveraging DeFi in Crypto Trading

Decentralized Finance (DeFi) has revolutionized the way we interact with financial services, offering new opportunities for traders. This chapter introduces the concept of DeFi and its core components, including decentralized exchanges (DEXs), lending and borrowing platforms, and yield farming. By understanding these elements, traders can leverage DeFi to enhance their trading strategies and maximize returns.

Decentralized exchanges, such as Uniswap and SushiSwap, play a pivotal role in the DeFi ecosystem. This chapter explains how DEXs operate, their advantages over centralized exchanges, and the unique opportunities they present for traders. Topics such as liquidity provision, automated market makers (AMMs), and impermanent loss are discussed to provide a comprehensive understanding of DEXs.

Lending and borrowing platforms, such as Aave and Compound, enable users to earn interest on their crypto holdings or borrow assets without traditional intermediaries. This chapter explores the mechanics of these platforms, the benefits of participating in lending and borrowing, and the risks involved. By incorporating these platforms into their trading strategies, traders can optimize their capital efficiency and generate additional income.

Yield farming, a popular DeFi activity, involves providing liquidity to various protocols in exchange for rewards. This chapter delves into the intricacies of yield farming, including the different strategies, potential returns, and associated risks. By understanding yield farming, traders can take advantage of the lucrative opportunities it offers while managing the inherent risks.

10

Chapter 10: Security Best Practices for Crypto Traders

Security is paramount in the world of cryptocurrency trading. This chapter provides a comprehensive guide to best practices for safeguarding digital assets and personal information. Topics such as securing wallets, enabling two-factor authentication (2FA), and using hardware wallets are covered in detail. By following these best practices, traders can minimize the risk of hacks and theft.

Securing wallets is a critical aspect of protecting digital assets. This chapter explains the different types of wallets, including hot wallets, cold wallets, and hardware wallets, and their respective security features. Practical tips for choosing and using wallets securely are provided to help traders safeguard their funds.

Two-factor authentication (2FA) adds an extra layer of security to trading accounts. This chapter discusses the importance of 2FA, how to set it up, and the best practices for using it effectively. By enabling 2FA, traders can significantly reduce the risk of unauthorized access to their accounts.

Hardware wallets, such as Ledger and Trezor, offer the highest level of security for storing cryptocurrencies. This chapter explains the benefits of using hardware wallets, how they work, and how to set them up. By using hardware wallets, traders can protect their assets from online threats and ensure their long-term security.

11

Chapter 11: Tax Implications and Legal Considerations

Understanding the tax implications and legal considerations of cryptocurrency trading is crucial for traders. This chapter provides an overview of the tax treatment of cryptocurrencies in various jurisdictions and the legal aspects of trading digital assets. By being aware of these factors, traders can ensure compliance and avoid potential legal issues.

The tax treatment of cryptocurrencies varies widely across countries. This chapter explores the different approaches to taxing cryptocurrency transactions, including capital gains tax, income tax, and value-added tax (VAT). Practical examples and case studies are provided to illustrate how these taxes apply to different trading activities.

Legal considerations are also essential for cryptocurrency traders. This chapter discusses the regulatory landscape for cryptocurrencies, including anti-money laundering (AML) and know-your-customer (KYC) requirements. By understanding the legal framework, traders can operate within the law and avoid potential penalties.

This chapter also covers the importance of keeping accurate records of all cryptocurrency transactions. Proper record-keeping can help traders track their gains and losses, calculate taxes accurately, and provide documentation in case of audits. Practical tips for maintaining records and using software tools to simplify the process are provided.

12

Chapter 12: Future Trends and Innovations in Crypto Trading

The world of cryptocurrency trading is constantly evolving, with new trends and innovations shaping the market. This chapter explores the future of crypto trading, including emerging technologies, regulatory developments, and market trends. By staying informed about these trends, traders can position themselves for long-term success.

Emerging technologies, such as decentralized finance (DeFi), non-fungible tokens (NFTs), and layer 2 solutions, are transforming the crypto landscape. This chapter discusses the potential impact of these technologies on trading strategies and market dynamics. By understanding these innovations, traders can identify new opportunities and stay ahead of the curve.

Regulatory developments are another critical factor influencing the future of crypto trading. This chapter examines the evolving regulatory landscape and its implications for traders. By staying informed about regulatory changes, traders can adapt their strategies and ensure compliance with the law.

Market trends, such as the increasing adoption of cryptocurrencies by institutions and the growing popularity of decentralized exchanges, are shaping the future of crypto trading. This chapter explores these trends and their potential impact on the market. By understanding these trends, traders can make informed decisions and capitalize on emerging opportunities.

Finally, this chapter emphasizes the importance of continuous learning and staying updated with the latest developments in the crypto space. The cryptocurrency market is dynamic and rapidly changing, and traders must stay informed to remain competitive. By embracing new technologies, adapting to regulatory changes, and staying ahead of market trends, traders can achieve long-term success in the world of cryptocurrency trading.

www.ingramcontent.com/pod-product-compliance
Ingram Content Group UK Ltd.
Pitfield, Milton Keynes, MK11 3LW, UK
UKHW021015050225
454710UK00012B/673